What's in this book?

"She asked me 'Is mummy sick because I was naughty?'"
Colin

As big as it gets

Help and support ... for parents and children

We have written this booklet to help parents help their children. Perhaps as you are reading this you are thinking "But I am fighting this illness. I will have every treatment I can. The children don't need to know what is happening. This booklet is not for me". If so, please think again. If the illness is serious, if it will change you in some way, if it is causing you to feel worried or stressed, then it will affect your children.

There are no 'right' answers, but there are options – and there are questions your children are likely to ask. There are reactions – situations you can handle and resolve. There are signs that can warn you to seek professional help.

Families come in all shapes and sizes and no family is like any other. You may have a supportive partner or one who finds it hard to face what is happening. You may be facing this challenge on your own with children.

Encouraging resilience, strength and confidence

This booklet has been written so your child can feel resilient and strong, and confident enough to share the natural feelings of loss when someone they love is seriously ill.

Some of the ideas and conversations may feel almost unbearably challenging to you as a protective and loving parent. However, every activity is included because we know it will help your child in the short and long term. Together, the ideas and activities will act as an 'emotional insurance policy' that you are putting in place should the worst happen – that is, if you don't pull through. But, like all insurance policies, it will not make it more likely to happen. Hopefully, it will mean that you can feel reassured that you have put tangible reminders in place that you love your children unconditionally and that it is not your choice to be ill. Trying to be emotionally available as a parent 'in sickness and in health' is never easy. Trust your instincts and confidence – after all, you know your children best.

Living in a different way

The reality of living with a serious illness, especially when the prognosis is not a good one, highlights the challenge of trying to live with uncertainty and maintaining hope. Involving children in such a complex emotional mix is daunting.

Increasingly, a diagnosis of something like cancer is more about a treatable illness than a terminal condition. A great number of people recover from cancer. Even those with a terminal prognosis are surviving longer. This raises the possibility of what Jane Tomlinson CBE described as "to live what life I have left in a different way".

Holding on to hope, and living each day to the full, inspires many people to feel they have choices at a time when they could easily feel helpless and alone. The ideas presented here simply encourage you to do this with your children at a time when your future health is uncertain.

"I remember the day I decided to tell them that the cancer had returned. I was in the kitchen stirring the spaghetti sauce. I wanted to keep moving that spoon forever. When I stopped I knew I would tell them something that would change their lives. If I didn't tell them would it make it less real? I knew that wasn't an option and I dreaded the questions that could follow … but wanted to be both honest and hopeful. They deserved that at least. We cried, we laughed … we were in this together. This was the first day of the rest of our lives …" Jenni, recalling the evening she told her teenage twins that she had secondary bone and liver cancer.

Dealing with the truth

Children have an ability to deal with the truth that adults often underestimate. Not knowing can make them feel anxious or confused.

Pretending to your child in any way will inevitably make things worse. The belief that children don't know what is happening is perhaps in itself misleading. Children almost always know or, at least, know 'something'. Partial or inaccurate information can be more worrying than the truth. If other people know about your illness, you may worry that your children may hear about it from someone other than you. Even very sad truths will be better than the uncertainty of not knowing what is happening. We cannot stop children feeling sad, but if we share our feelings and give them information, we can support them in their sadness.

"If I tell Sarah I've got this, that means I really do. How can I fight this thing and keep a positive attitude, if I tell the very person who could make me cry?" Pete

Balancing hope and honesty

Maintaining both **hope** and **honesty** is crucial at this time. Some parents believe that if they do not talk about the illness with their children, it will not touch them.

However, if a parent cannot and does not acknowledge that they are ill, then they certainly cannot acknowledge the feelings, thoughts and responses that come with it. Many adults feel that as long as the experience is not given a name or discussed, children will go on with their lives as though nothing is happening.

Needing to know what's going on

Children often surprise us with their capacity to absorb new experiences and difficult thoughts. Children need to understand that hope, fear, anger, sadness and intense love are all appropriate feelings when a person they care about is seriously ill.

One mother decided not to tell her nine-year-old son that she had leukaemia. However, he overheard his father talking to a family friend on the phone. He was furious and upset at being excluded.

This boy needed to know what was happening in order to make sense of the experience and his parents' reactions. Being included in future conversations made him feel stronger and more involved.

Working through our own anxieties and discomfort

Our difficulty in talking with children often stems from our own anxieties and discomfort. Recognising your own fears, concerns and hopes for the future may be an important first step in feeling ready to involve your children. We all seek to be in control. To be in a place of uncertainty and to allow your children to join you in that place of uncertainty takes great courage.

It is important to recognise that we are looking at the rest of your children's lives. If they are 'protected' from the truth, they will learn a lifelong lesson of distrust. There may be nothing more important in their lives than continuing to trust the people they love most – the parent who is sick and the parent or family who will continue to care for them.

If you have a partner, you may find that you have different approaches to discussing the illness and to involving the children in what is happening. Every family is unique and it helps to talk through the meaning of your illness at this particular time for your particular family. A conversation with one of the helplines listed on page 42 of this booklet may help both of you. Non-talkers won't magically transform into sharers. It will, however, be helpful to your children if you reach a point where you can both agree that the children should be involved – and to what extent.

"They didn't tell me anything. She's **my** mother, and I want to know what's going on!" Luke

"The illness put a great strain on our relationship. Gradually we had to learn to live for today, not tomorrow." Jane

"Somehow I felt as though I must carry on. After all, I wasn't sick myself and I suppose I thought 'men should cope'.

I didn't have cancer and have to deal with all the treatments. Jane was coping so well – she was very courageous. I was breaking up inside, but trying not to show it.

My GP was great: he's a father too. He asked all the right questions and soon I found myself telling him about the things that were bothering me. We chatted regularly after that. I couldn't have come through this without him." Mike

Telling the children

Making a start

What, when and how you tell your children about your illness will depend on many things, including:

- the age of the children
- the nature of the prognosis – if you are likely, or not likely, to recover
- your children's previous experience of loss.

What and when to tell

It can be helpful to think of the process as a little bit like putting together a jigsaw. Younger children may not need to have all the pieces from the beginning. Even older children may not be able to handle too much information at one time.

Children's increasing understanding works both ways of course. Older children will be better able to understand what you tell them about your illness but may also be more concerned because they understand.

You know your children best, so you can best judge how much information to share – and when. If they have had previous experience of other losses (such as deaths of important people or pets, changes of schools,

divorce, friends moving away), you may find that their reactions to what you say are more intense.

It will, of course, help if you can choose a time when there will be enough time to talk, to answer questions and provide reassurance. However, children's questions come at unpredictable times and you may have to balance the need to get to school on time with the opportunity for a family conversation.

There are three things to tell your children:

- mum or dad is seriously ill
- the name of the illness
- your best understanding of what may happen.

This usually leads to important questions such as:

- Did I do anything to cause it?
- Can I catch it?
- Who will do the things that dad/mum does for me now they are sick?
- Will they die?

You may worry that telling children about the illness is likely to lead to difficult questions. But encouraging

questions – and taking them seriously – will reassure them and help them to feel included. It's quite normal for children to ask all sorts of questions ranging from "Does it hurt?" to "Can I still go to my new school?" It is important that they understand that they did nothing to cause the illness, that they can't catch it and that plans are in place for the future.

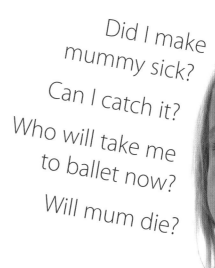

Did I make mummy sick?
Can I catch it?
Who will take me to ballet now?
Will mum die?

Even though dad will have to go to hospital every day for his treatment, you can still go to the clubs after school and Earl's mum has said you can go to their house for tea on Mondays.

If you can't answer a question exactly, it's fine to say "I don't know". In fact, this answer is much better than a guess or making something up. If you are unsure about an answer you might say:

That's a difficult question – to be honest, I'm not sure I know the answer. I need to find out more from mum's doctor before I can answer that.

And then it's important to make sure you do this and come back to them with an answer when you have one.

Choosing the right words

It's hard to work out the best words on the spot, so you might prefer to rehearse what you want to say first and prepare some possible answers to their questions. Try and use words the children will understand. Pictures and some of the books on pages 44 and 45 may help you explain an illness that can't always be seen on the outside.

One explanation to a younger child might sound like this:

Remember I told you dad was not well and the doctor wanted to try to find out what was wrong? To do this dad went to the hospital and they took a small piece out of the lump in his tummy and looked at it very carefully with a microscope. Well, today dad and I went back to the hospital and they told us dad is ill because he has an illness inside his tummy called cancer.

It's generally a good idea to tell children the name of the illness – they are going to hear (or overhear) the word a lot and it is better for them to know what it is called rather than confusing euphemisms.

It's also worth explaining that illness can make everyone a bit more emotional than usual. Warn them that mum or dad may seem distant or upset – or even grumpy – sometimes. And warn children that they may feel a bit left out for a while because the person who is sick needs lots of time and attention.

When an operation or further treatment is necessary

If the person is likely to get better, you can give a fairly positive answer:

Because of mum's illness the doctors are going to do an operation to try and fix what is wrong with her. They think that this operation will make her better.

The doctors think it will help dad to have some strong medicine called chemotherapy to fight the cancer. Although this medicine will help him, it will also make him feel sick and tired for a while before he starts to feel better again.

Reassure the children that you'll tell them exactly what is happening, and that you'll try to keep life as normal as possible.

This is also the time to prepare them for possible physical changes, such as hair loss (see page 16).

If treatment has not been successful

Depending on the ages of your children, this will be the time to give them more 'pieces of the jigsaw'. Older children may ask for more information and will already be thinking about what this might mean for everyone in the family.

The doctors are trying very hard to make mum better and it's a real shame that the operation wasn't completely successful. But sometimes the illness she has is hard to make better.

The doctors are thinking about what treatment to try next but just now we are not really sure what will happen.

We've got a hospital appointment next Tuesday.

Riding the emotional rollercoaster

> "We often felt they weren't interested in what we were saying – but I'm sure that's a defence and, like us, children need time to absorb what's been said." Don

Reacting to the news

Children can react very differently to the news that someone is seriously ill. They may be very upset and may cry or be angry. However, don't be surprised if they ask to go back to their TV programme, computer game or simply ask "What's for tea?" This doesn't mean that they don't care – but it's sometimes hard for them to understand and respond to what's been said straight away. It can take children a while to express their fears and uncertainties after hearing the news.

You may also find that the experience of telling your children suddenly makes what is happening feel more real to you. Be prepared for your own reactions and seek out those who can support you at this time. Allow yourself to be supported by family and friends.

The rollercoaster

"When I told the children their dad had gone to the hospice, my seven-year-old looked terrified and tearful. Some days later I learnt from his older sister that Sean had thought he might have to be adopted as mum would now have to go to live with dad at the hospice. Slowly I allowed myself to see the last year through his confused, bewildered eyes. I realised then how little I had prepared and involved him in what was the biggest event of his life. All he knew was that family life was under threat; his playmate dad couldn't play any more – no-one had thought to explain to him that his dad had cancer, was having complicated treatment and how worried we all felt when the pain required hospice admission. The older children knew a bit more, but as a family we were so busy protecting each other that we somehow stopped talking about the important stuff. The nurse helped me to find the words to explain and to find out what Sean was really thinking and feeling. We held a family meeting at the hospice. We cried, we laughed, we hugged – the Robinsons were back on track. Together we could deal with the rollercoaster ride ahead." Mona

Give and take

Living with a serious illness can be exhausting for everyone concerned. The mixture of uncertainty and hope can be draining, and treatment can be very tiring.

Warn your children that the people around them are likely to be distracted, emotional and irritable. That's natural. This is a time in the family for give and take, and for not taking things too personally.

Everyone will be on a short fuse. Praise children who want to help and be involved. At the same time, show understanding to those children who need to be distracted and distanced from the day-to-day reality. There are some activities (see section starting on page 23) which can help you show your children what they mean to you – in turn, this will help them feel more confident.

Children's feelings

Children may show little or no immediate reaction to the news, but they often show they are upset in other ways.

- Some children may cling to you too much, terrified that something will happen if they are not there.
- Some children may withdraw from you, unconsciously trying to become more independent.
- Some children may feel sorry for themselves, and then feel guilty that they are not supportive of their parent.
- Some children may decide to be especially good, setting themselves impossibly high standards.
- Some children may show their frustration by being unco-operative, dismissive and angry at everything.
- Some children may be quite 'hyper', laughing and over-excitable as a way to disguise real feelings or their lack of understanding.
- Some children may experience minor physical symptoms which may be 'real' but brought on by stress, for example stomach and headaches.
- Some children may become a bit fixated, for example on washing their hands a lot because they are afraid they will 'catch' the cancer or illness too.
- Some children may regress, feeling vulnerable and 'little' inside. This may show itself in lack of concentration, bedwetting, sleep disturbances, thumb-sucking and temper tantrums.

All these feelings and reactions are natural and normal; let your child know that you understand them and are here to help them manage these feelings. Most of these feelings will settle with time. There are several activities described in this booklet (see section starting on page 23) that are designed to help children manage the uncertainty of family life when someone is seriously ill. Some of the activities can be good fun for both parents and children – humour and love are an excellent antidote to fear and anxiety.

You can also call one of the helplines on pages 42 and 43 for support and guidance over how your children are feeling and reacting to the illness of their parent.

"I was six years old when my dad told me that mum had incurable cancer … to my eternal shame I reacted by asking him for my pocket money." Amy

Coping with frustration

If their behaviour is out of control, your natural impulse might be to scream "Don't you know dad's sick? You are so thoughtless!" Instead, try saying it in a slightly different way, but with a firm grasp on giving children boundaries.

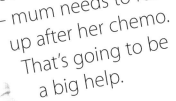

Look, just for a while I need you to think about being quiet – not running, not slamming things – mum needs to rest up after her chemo. That's going to be a big help.

A mother who developed cancer was still on chemotherapy and feeling very rough at the time of the following incident. She describes what happened after 11-year-old Tom had started to misbehave regularly:

> **"I remember so clearly my utter fury at Tom when he defied me and swore at me. I suppose I suddenly realised how far I'd let the discipline side of things slip. I really lost it and screamed at him. I think I was afraid my lovable boy was turning into a horrible brat. After I stopped shouting, Tom calmed down and became very cheerful and loving. I think children need to feel that someone other than themselves is in control."** Lena

Tom's recollection of the swearing incident was also interesting.

> **"Well, when mum heard me swear, she totally lost her temper. She screamed at me that she was in charge and I wasn't allowed to be rude! I went and got my school bag fast. I felt better than I had in a long time. I think now I was rude on purpose to see if mum was really in there. She was. We soon made up."** Tom

Children's needs

Very young children need security, security and security. Stick to the routines you have at nursery, meal times, sleep and bedtimes.

For school-aged children, try to maintain the activities they value and create opportunities for them to ask the questions that may be troubling them. They will also value the reassurance of a normal routine and also times when this is abandoned for something more important such as:

- a shared activity when 'mum is feeling better tonight'
- a game that lasts right to the end and not just till tea time
- an important conversation that needs to continue.

They will also appreciate reassurance about what might happen to them in the future. Even the children of two healthy parents are reassured to know who would look after them if anything happened.

> **"I've told them that Val and I have every intention of living to see our grandchildren but that, if anything happens, their aunt and uncle would look after them."** Simon

How teenagers may react

Teenagers also vary in how they react to a parent's serious illness. Many may become even less communicative, picking up on family tension but saying very little.

They may feel they want to stay around home a lot and help out, especially if they have younger brothers and sisters. Or they may feel that they'd rather be anywhere else, so want to stay out with friends and try to forget what is happening. They may find it hard or even impossible to talk to you, preferring to get their support from their friends, and they may find things like details of your illness embarrassing. Normal teenage behaviour can seem less tolerable when someone is ill.

Encourage your doctor or nurse to talk directly with them so they feel part of what is happening. The most important thing is for the family to try to keep talking together and for them to know they are valued, can be involved and will be trusted with information when they choose to have it.

Some teenagers may try to escape from their worries through excessive drinking and drugs or through self-harm. They are expressing their pain and overwhelming emotions and these need to be acknowledged. The opportunity is then there to talk about other, less harmful ways to express some of these fierce feelings. It may also be the time for some outside help.

Getting professional help

Most families can cope with a serious illness and, if they can talk about what is happening and how they feel about it, they often surprise themselves by how well they actually cope. It is often when families can't talk that they find they have difficulties. So, above all, try to keep talking to each other, even if your communication starts off with 'post-it' notes on pillows, bedroom doors or fridges.

Parents sometimes think their children need professional help as soon as a serious illness is diagnosed. This may be because they feel helpless faced with children's reactions to the news. Most families somehow find the resources to support each other, even through the most difficult of times.

However, you may find that some difficulties persist or get worse. In this case, talk it over with one of the helplines on pages 42 and 43, your family doctor, or staff at a hospital or hospice. They will be able to help you clarify if a referral to a child specialist is the best way forward.

I know you're scared. I'm scared too. That's why we argue sometimes. Love you – Mum x

The role of schools

Making school a positive part of the journey

School plays a familiar, routine part in children's lives. Even when someone in the family is very ill, many children still want to go to school because it gives them a sense of stability. Some will also see school as a place to forget what is happening to their parent for a few hours. Others will feel too anxious and sad to concentrate. Some will not want to go to school at all. This may be because they don't want to miss something important at home or because they want to be around if they are needed. Others may worry that they'll get upset and embarrassed in front of their friends. It is important that the school and all the teachers who come into contact with the child know what is happening so that they can understand when someone is struggling and be prepared to offer support.

You may feel it is hard to talk to teachers about the illness. But the more teachers know about what is happening at home, the more they can help. Some head teachers, but not all, will really understand the journey you are all on and will actively know what is required to make school a positive part of that journey. Some, however, will not. As a first step, you could ask them to read this booklet and then arrange to have a conversation such as this:

> **Thanks for seeing us all today, Mrs Jordan. We wanted you to know that our family is in a really tough place right now. Recently we heard from the hospital that my cancer has returned. I had treatment for lung cancer six years ago when Milly and Harry were in primary school. It's been a great shock as I now need to start treatment again and there are no guarantees how things will turn out. The cancer has spread to my brain. We wanted you to be aware so you can give Milly and Harry the support they will need to keep being successful at school. They have come up with two great ideas – firstly, that we send an update e-mail to you every week or fortnight and secondly they have both chosen one of their teachers who they each feel they can really trust to talk to while I'm having treatment. Does that sound like a good idea to you?**

"He was very distracted in class. I had no idea his father was so ill. He never told us and I never thought to ask." Tim, a teacher

Understanding the pressures

If you do happen to have an understanding head teacher then consider yourself lucky – but don't expect it. Serious illness means different things to different people at different points in their lives. Some teachers will have had their own personal experiences which may leave them feeling awkward and unable to respond in a way you would find helpful. It doesn't necessarily mean they don't care; it may just mean that they feel uncomfortable responding to a child's emotional needs. Perhaps there is another teacher who could help.

Persevere with communication as the school really does need to understand the on-going pressures that your children will be facing.

At Winston's Wish we regularly receive calls to our helpline from teachers who are keen to do the right thing but want to check out their approach, for example when planning activities around Father's Day or Mother's Day or when balancing understanding a child's situation with the impact of their disruptive behaviour. Your child's teacher may like to have our helpline number (08452 03 04 05).

"When her mum's having treatment, she sometimes needs to talk and I try to make time at break." Alan, a teacher

Preparing for change

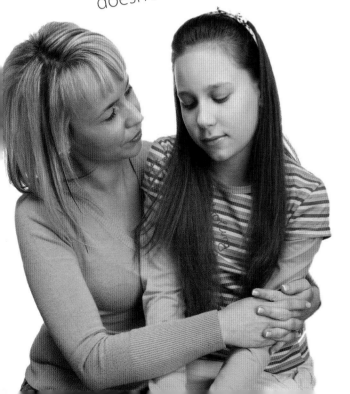

Dad's very ill, so he might be tired and might sleep a lot and not do very much. Being very ill makes you weak, but that doesn't mean he doesn't care about you.

Explaining the side-effects

"I wasn't aware that John had been so affected by the changes he saw in his dad which were caused by the drugs – perhaps because I saw him every day, I didn't notice them so much. John came home from college and seemed really shocked by Dean's weight and hair loss."
Corinne

"My dad has cancer, and he was in hospital for a long time. When he finally got to come home he was really sick. I had to help him up the stairs because he was so weak. It was strange because he had always been so big and strong, and now he was weak. It bothered me."
Richard

Some illnesses and their treatments can change people's appearance. They may lose weight or lose their hair and they may have tubes connected to various parts of their body. You need to warn children if a parent looks changed and give them a simple explanation why this has happened.

If someone is very sick, it may be worth taking a photo to prepare the children in advance. Try to reassure the children that the person is just the same, even though they may look different.

It may also help to talk about some of the side-effects the medicine might be causing.

Dad's medicine makes sure he doesn't have any pain. But the doctor told me it sometimes makes him feel woozy and he might say things that come out all funny. That's because of the medicine – but don't worry, he's not in pain.

When someone is ill they often do very little because their bodies aren't working well. They don't need to eat very often or do much. The medicine will make sure dad is not in too much pain.

Overwhelming tiredness

This is an excerpt from a mother's blog diary which gives a sense of the exhaustion that many parents feel from cancer treatments.

"I've been very tired lately and I seem to have spent the last week in and out of bed during the afternoons. It's not really fair on the kids but I just can't help it. Freddie wrote me a note saying that he wished I wouldn't go to bed so much and that when he asks me to get up he wishes I would. He says that he gets bored when I'm in bed! What can I do? I'm forever being told that I don't rest enough and should ask for more help and then when I do listen to my body I get moaned at. Oh well, such is life when you've got kids!" Dawn, www.wigstowishes.org.uk

When the children want to visit the hospital or hospice

Often the well or sick parent may think:

I don't want them to see me (or mum/dad) like this.

I don't want them to remember me (or her/him) in this way.

I don't want them to be frightened or have nightmares.

If the children themselves are asking to visit, try to put these thoughts aside and consider the benefits of not shutting them out at this critical point. Children may be thinking:

Why can't I see my mum/dad? I really need to see them.

Do they look like a monster then?

Don't they want to see me? Don't they love me any more?

Prepare your children for what their parent will look like and how the room is set up. Describe the colours, furniture, equipment, smells, even the pictures on the wall.

It can help children to have a task to perform, such as to fill up the flower vases, offer their parent a drink or draw a picture that can remain when they leave.

When children do not want to visit

On the other hand, some children may feel that they do not want to visit their sick parent. This can be very upsetting for everyone involved but insisting is probably counter-productive. Instead, develop ways to keep close links between them and the person who is ill. Phone calls are important. When even this is difficult, they can send in cards, bunches of flowers picked from the garden, the latest football scores, photos of the family pet, a CD of music.

Even the very briefest of visits can help both the child and the ill parent to maintain a connection, for example a quick dash in and out with the newspaper.

"She couldn't bear to see Euan like that and I couldn't force her. It was breaking his heart though. My friend helped her make a card which she just managed to hand over and then Joy took her down to the hospital shop to buy her some sweets and Euan a magazine. She gave it to her dad (and one of her sweets) before she hurried back out. It meant all the world to him – and later it meant all the world to her too." Kate

Staying away from home

"Sometimes when they wanted me to stay with Auntie Mary, I'd make out I felt sick or had a really bad tummy ache so I could stay at home. I wanted to be at home with dad in case he needed anything." Jamie

You might feel that your children would be better off staying with relatives or friends because you're trying so hard to cope with the extra pressures that illness brings and have so little time to look after your children. But even if things are very hard at home, many children don't want to be separated from their immediate family and find it quite scary to be away at such a time. If they are sent somewhere else they may worry that things are actually much worse than they thought, or that they've been so naughty that they can't be allowed to stay.

However, the illness, symptom or treatment may be so severe that the only solution is for the children to stay somewhere else – at least for short periods of time. If you decide this is the best option, work out ways to stay in touch. Organise regular visits, phone calls, texts, e-mails or send letters, web cam or MSN messages to keep children up to date with what is happening. If at all possible, try to give children an idea of when they may be able to come home.

I've arranged for you and Zack to stay with granny for four days. As you know, dad is really sick right now and I need to spend all my time getting his special meals and medicine, taking him to the toilet and giving him a bath. He also needs me at night as the pain and his coughing are quite bad then. I'm worried that I can't look after you all as well as I would like, so granny has offered to help out. This week you will go to her house and then next week she will come up to our house to help out here. I'll ring you every day you're at granny's to let you know how things are going. You'll be back in time to see your mates on Thursday.

If recovery is unlikely

If you are certain a parent is not going to recover

If you have reached a point when your health is deteriorating to such a degree that you know you will die, then the most difficult conversation of all will need to take place.

If you can summon up the strength, then it really is best for children to hear this news from the people they trust most – their parents. When hope is taken away, then it is fairly inevitable that those who have been clinging to that life raft will feel cast adrift and desperately sad, even angry. Children are no different.

Hannah, do you remember that we agreed that I would always let you know what the doctors said about my illness? And that I wouldn't pretend to you – even if that meant that the news wasn't always good? Well, today I spoke with Dr Khan at the hospital and he told me that the cancer has got much worse. He does not think he can make me better now. He thinks that I may not have very long to live and that is why I am so sleepy ...

For an older child who you feel can handle the uncertainty, you may decide to involve them with more information.

"Telling the children that I was likely to die was the hardest thing I ever had to do. I hope it didn't come as a total shock as we had tried to involve them along the way. Nathan left the room in tears and Amy couldn't look at me – I think she was in shock. I just hugged her." Rachel

The doctors have tried all they can – the operation, all the chemo – but some cancers just can't be cured however hard the doctors try. We know now that he will die. We hope we will have a few more months with dad. But we don't think he will be alive for your next birthday. He will seem quite well to begin with and the doctors will make sure he is not in pain.

"Even though Dave has just started another round of chemo to help with the lung secondaries, I realised that underneath all my many brave faces I was terrified that he might die. I felt that if we talked about it, it would make it more likely to happen and he would think I had given up. Then, last night we had the most open discussion ever. I felt so close to him and it somehow felt OK for me to share my fears with him. He had been thinking about it a lot too. He told me some of his wishes if he suddenly became very ill. Today it was like a weight was off our shoulders; we had gone there, we can go there again but we don't have to spend all our time thinking about it. Today we booked a weekend in Devon – Dave has more energy and he wants to do things. I feel stronger too and the kids can sense that mum and dad are a team again." Lizzie

If the illness becomes truly terminal, children may become less comfortable about asking questions. If this is the case, you can help them by taking the initiative – ask them how much they want to know. How families respond at this point varies enormously and this may be a good time to call the Winston's Wish helpline (on 08452 03 04 05) to discuss your individual concerns.

A father told a hospice nurse he didn't think his wife understood that she was dying. **"I don't think she can handle this."** He felt he couldn't tell their children. He thought it would be disloyal while his wife still kept hoping for a cure and that the children shouldn't talk about death. Later on, when his teenage daughter visited the hospice, she told the same nurse **"I know mum is dying – we've talked about it"**. It turned out that Becky was helping her mum to bath one day and she had said **"I'm not sure I'm going to make it this time Becks – I think I'm dying"**.

The nurse asked Becky if she thought they could share that with dad. Becky looked startled and unsure. **"I'm not sure dad could handle that."**

The family still tended to avoid conversations with the 'D word' but they were eventually able to acknowledge that Becky's mother was dying, and to support each other.

When death is imminent

Children need the opportunity of these last times together. The physical situation may be daunting, and may be frightening, but your children can get past this. They're trying to reach the real parent who they love – and their love goes way beyond what their parent looks like or acts like.

> Mum has tried so hard to beat this illness. The doctors and everyone at the hospital have tried so hard too. Now it is time for her to die. She's not in pain. The doctors think it may be in the next few days but it could be sooner. Although she'll be very weak and sleepy we'll try to make mum comfortable. Her breathing will gradually slow down and after a while her heart will stop. The nurse told me that mum is unlikely to be able to talk any more but she may be able to hear us if we want to say anything.

The last days of a parent's life will inevitably be heartbreakingly sad. Yet with the right help and support, children will also be able to look back on those days as being full of love and precious closeness. In time, they will be able to remember and smile about mum or dad's **life** and not only think of their death.

Even if mum can't talk to you, or say thanks for the card you have made, she will still know that you are here and that you love her.

Living for today

The last few pages were hard to write and must have been almost unbearably difficult to read.

However, facing your very worst fear may at least enable you to discuss it with your partner or someone you trust. It is so important that you find ways of responding to this fear so that your spirit and love for the people you care about can shine through.

The activities on the next few pages should help you to feel less overwhelmed by the fear, cope with the good days and the bad days, and live life to the full right now. The ideas will probably be best completed on days when you feel stronger and have some energy.

Above all, we hope you will be able to enjoy family life – because **the spirit of family life is stronger than any illness and it can last forever**.

Practical ways to support children

The activities on the following pages are designed to help children manage the uncertainty of family life when someone is seriously ill.

Understanding what's happening: telling their story

Telling their story of what is happening in the family by drawing or writing it out on a 'film strip' is a creative way to understand the child's world, while also feeding in accurate information. In this way, you can find out what a child knows (or believes is real) before launching into telling them more information.

This activity often works best with someone outside the immediate family setting it up and prompting, with the children drawing or writing their words on the strip. Parents can then come and listen, and respond to the children's experience of the serious illness journey. Many parents find it very moving and helpful to witness the depth and understanding revealed.

In this film strip, a boy expresses his thoughts and feelings about his mother's illness.

"From hearing them tell the story of my illness and the effect on the family through the film strip, I realised that the children had reserves of strength and character that were truly amazing. Overnight it seemed to allow them to become more self-sufficient, have greater self-confidence and show me that we were in this together. I am so proud of them, and now they know that too!" Nisa

Telling your story

YOU'LL NEED:
Scissors
Coloured pens/pencils
Sticky tape

YOU COULD ALSO USE:
Photos
Glue

WHAT TO DO:
When someone important is ill, you can sometimes feel really worried and confused. It might often go round and round in your head, popping into your imagination at all sorts of moments. This activity helps you think about life before the diagnosis and then helps you show the journey for your family as you understand it. It helps you to take some control over when you 'view your story'.

Step 1: Get some coloured pens and pencils and make a film strip. (You may need to copy this sheet a few times.) Stick the sheets together to form a long strip. Decide what you might include on this film strip. Think of it as a movie of how your life has changed since mum or dad got ill. Include all the important things that have happened to you.

Step 2: In the first frames write about or draw pictures of family life before the illness, then show what happened next, treatment, hospital visits and anything else that is important in your family at this time.

You may want to include pictures or words. Include as much information as is comfortable, but make sure that you have a full story on your film strip. You may need to ask other people questions to get a full picture. Give equal space to each section of your story. Don't focus too much on one scene, or ignore another part.

Step 3: Finish off with details of how life is now, who is important to you, what has changed and what the future might be. Blank frames at the end can be left to be filled in when your parent recovers – or if they need more treatment.

Step 4: Roll up your film strip and keep it in a safe place. You could use it to help you tell your story to other people.

NOW YOU HAVE FINISHED TELLING YOUR STORY, YOU CAN SHARE IT WITH OTHER PEOPLE.

Remembering good times, accepting tough times too: memory stones

"When I'm having a bad day I sometimes look at my stones to help me feel better. The one that makes me smile is my blue gemstone. It reminds me how much fun we used to have on holiday, swimming in the sea and just being an ordinary family."

Ryan

A simple bag of three stones may be a useful way to have a really meaningful conversation with your children.

Encouraging a child's curiosity is often a good place to start. The **smooth pebble** is there because even though times have been hard with mum or dad's illness – ordinary everyday life still goes on. Explain to them that the **rough sharp rock** is there to represent the difficult and hard times. And finally the **gemstone** is there to remind them of the really special times together. The first two stones can usually be found in a garden or park. Gemstones can be found at craft or gift shops. See page 46 for a special set you can buy. If you have more than one child you could choose a different gemstone and different bag design for each child.

Encourage your children to hold each stone in turn and give examples of feelings and events that they would attach to the different stones. You can also share your own. Together you will find that using this simple bag of stones can help break the conspiracy of silence that sometimes creeps in when tough stuff happens in families.

When having a tough day the stones can be a useful way to start a conversation: for example **"Does the rough rock feel particularly sharp today?"**

Memory stones

YOU'LL NEED:
A smooth ordinary pebble
A rough sharp rock
A shiny gemstone
Somewhere to keep these stones

WHAT TO DO:
In every relationship we have, there are ordinary, difficult and special moments. Ordinary moments and memories may be that the person likes two sugars in their coffee, or always walks you to school. There will also be some feelings and memories that are difficult to think about – for example, when you first heard that mum or dad was ill – and these can hurt and feel painful. The special memories could be the holidays you have been on, watching films together or buying sweets on a Friday. This activity will help you to balance all these ordinary, difficult, and special moments and memories.

Step 1: Find somewhere to keep your stones. This could be a small bag or box.

Step 2: You will need three stones. One needs to be ordinary, smooth and round, like a pebble. The second needs to be a rough stone with sharp jagged edges. The third needs to be special, like a gemstone.

Step 3: Spend time holding each stone. First hold the ordinary smooth pebble. Think of some everyday thoughts or memories you have of the person who is ill. Now hold the rough stone. Are there some memories or thoughts which are hard to think about and feel painful? Maybe there are things that you wish were different. Finally, hold the gemstone. Think of the special moments and times that you have shared together.

Step 4: Keep the stones together to remind you that different thoughts and memories can be held alongside one another.

smooth pebble

rough rock

shiny gemstone

MOST RELATIONSHIPS HAVE GOOD TIMES AND BAD TIMES. USE THESE STONES TO REPRESENT ALL YOUR DIFFERENT MEMORIES AND THOUGHTS. THINK MOST ABOUT THE ONES THAT HELP YOU TO FEEL CLOSE TO THE PERSON WHO IS SICK.

Expressing emotions: feelings jar

If we do not acknowledge that there is a serious illness in the family, then we certainly cannot acknowledge the feelings that go with it. Some adults feel that as long as it is not given a name, or discussed, children will go on with their lives as though nothing has happened.

Children need to understand that fear, love, anger and sadness are all appropriate feelings when a person they love is ill.

This activity can work in two ways. Either the child can make a feelings jar or you may want to suggest you each make one and then compare jars – and your thoughts on the feelings – together. It becomes a safe way for a sick or well parent to talk more openly about really important feelings. Remaining close, providing comfort and showing that they are central in your life are powerful gifts to give to children.

Five feelings are selected: for example anger, fear, love, sadness and hope. Give each feeling a colour. Then ask for examples of what thoughts or situations trigger these feelings. Here are some examples of colours, feelings and thoughts from Leona, aged 10, whose mum has advanced multiple sclerosis.

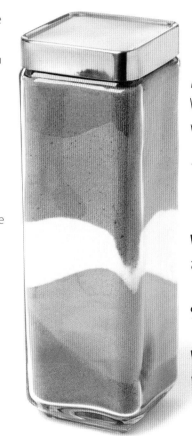

Anger "Why did my mum have to get MS? It's not fair. I hate it and wish it would go away. I feel angry when my mates discuss what their mum has been doing. They're lucky."

Love "I love my mum, her smile, her hugs, her pasta bake and chocolate brownies."

Fear "I am very worried that mum finds it hard to breathe at night. I am also scared that I might have to move school."

Sadness "I feel sad when I think mum may not get better."

Hope "I hope that mum will be well enough to walk at my sports day."

Feelings jar

YOU'LL NEED:

A small clean jar with a screw-top lid

Packet of table salt

Coloured chalks or pastels

Cotton wool ball

Five pieces of A4 paper and one small piece of paper

WHAT TO DO:

Each different colour in your feelings jar will represent a thought or feeling that you have had since someone in your family became ill. Whether happy or sad, they are important feelings to you.

Step 1: Think about five feelings you have.

Step 2: Begin by thinking of one thought that goes with each of the five feelings. Write these down on the small piece of paper.

Step 3: Decide on a colour for each feeling and mark that colour next to the feeling on your paper.

Step 4: Fill a small jar right up to the brim with salt, making sure it is jammed full. This gives you the exact amount of salt needed. Then tip the salt out of the jar into five piles on the five pieces of paper. Each of these piles will represent a feeling, so you could make them equal in size, or if some feelings are more significant, put more salt in that pile.

Step 5: Pick a coloured chalk or pastel and start to rub it into one pile of salt. As you rub it in, the salt will begin to turn that colour. Keep rubbing in a circular motion until it is the colour you want – the longer you rub, the more vibrant the colour.

Step 6: Once you have coloured all five piles of salt, carefully tip them into the jar. You can do this in straight layers, or diagonal ones, in thin strips or large ones – it is up to you. Once you have finished, tap the jar gently to settle the contents and add more salt if necessary. Then put a cotton wool ball on top and screw the lid back on tightly. The cotton wool ball stops the colours from mixing up as it forms a good seal.

Step 7: Share your jar with someone you feel safe with; tell them what the colours mean to you.

Step 8: Decide where you will keep your jar to remind you of all your different feelings.

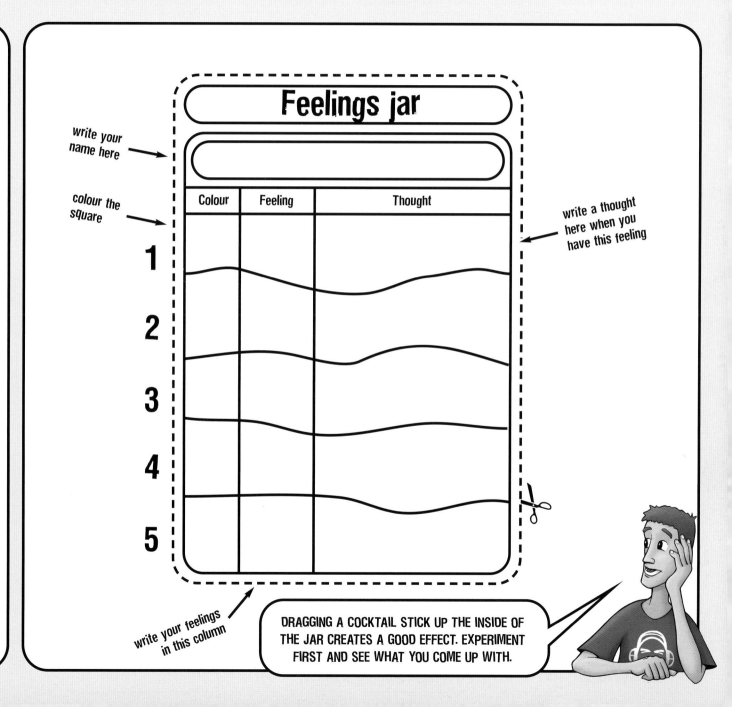

write your name here →

colour the square →

write a thought here when you have this feeling

Feelings jar

Colour	Feeling	Thought
1		
2		
3		
4		
5		

write your feelings in this column

DRAGGING A COCKTAIL STICK UP THE INSIDE OF THE JAR CREATES A GOOD EFFECT. EXPERIMENT FIRST AND SEE WHAT YOU COME UP WITH.

Treasuring stories: a special box

Children delight in rehearing and retelling stories in which they are the central character. They also love to feel loved.

When someone is ill, a special box can become an important way to pass on memories of treasured times to their children. You could use a shoe box or a biscuit tin. Winston's Wish sells specially made memory boxes (see page 46). A parent can make a box for a child or parents and children can make one together.

I found that on days after the chemo when I was often in bed, Matt would sometimes arrive in my bedroom with his box. We would spend hours just going over and over the same stories. The smile on his face helped to balance his worry that I was still sick. He didn't open the card that said 'I love you no matter what' but he knew it was there.

Objects can be labelled to prompt the kinds of stories that will mean a lot to children. A photo of the child with the parent who is ill can be stuck on the lid. This provides an important reminder of their connection and leads the way into a box full of stories. All sorts of things can be collected including tickets from places visited together, jewellery, cards, feathers found on a special walk, shells from a beach holiday, certificates and so on. A bottle of aftershave or perfume that dad or mum uses can be included and the child encouraged to spray it on a soft toy or even themselves. Our sense of smell is one of the most powerful ways to access memories so this can evoke strong feelings of connection with their parent when apart.

You might also write short stories or headlines for stories on a set of postcards or in a special memory book to go into the memory box.

This is dad's aftershave. You like a drop or two on your pillow when dad's away having treatment.

We picked up this shell when we crept out and walked on the beach at midnight. Do you remember the toast and hot chocolate we had afterwards?

Dear Matt, this was the lovely Mother's Day card you sent me. Always know I love you, no matter what....I am so proud of the person you are and the dreams you have for your sport. Love Mum x

My box of stories

YOU'LL NEED:

A box with a lid
Some things to remind you of the person who is ill

YOU COULD ALSO USE:

Tape
Glue
Pens
Things to personalise the outside of your box

WHAT TO DO:

In the box you can keep and treasure all kinds of things that remind you of the person who is ill. You can customise it to make it more personal, and fill it with photos, letters and objects that remind you of your experiences together. They may also want to add things to your special box.

Step 1: Find a box. It can be any type of box – it just has to be big enough for everything you want to keep in it.

Step 2: Decorate the box. You could use wrapping paper, pictures cut out of magazines, photos, stickers, shells or paints . . . be creative!

Step 3: Once the box is decorated, start filling it. You can put anything you want in it (as long as it will fit!) Check with other people in your family that it is OK with them for you to have things like photos and objects that belong to the person who is ill. Below are a few ideas of some things that you could include – but don't stop there – there's loads more.

Ideas for things to put in your box

Photos	Letters
CD of music	Postcards from holidays
Recording of you singing or talking together	Jewellery
	Items of clothing
Perfume or aftershave	Shells, cones, feathers
Cards	

Here are some ideas for things to put in your box:

THINK CAREFULLY ABOUT WHAT YOU PUT IN. MAKE SURE THERE ARE STORIES AND MEMORIES ATTACHED TO EACH ITEM. FOR EXAMPLE, AN OLD CINEMA TICKET MIGHT REMIND YOU OF YOUR FIRST TRIP TO THE CINEMA TOGETHER.

Coping with separation

Big one, small one

Younger children sometimes really struggle with separation from a parent who is having treatment or maybe having respite care in a hospice. One idea to respond to this 'separation anxiety' is to create a physical link between the child and the parent. For example, you could give them two matching soft toys – one '**Big**' and one '**Small**', for example two cats, two dragons, two teddies, two rabbits. What matters is a difference in size, so, for an older child, 'Big' need not be large and 'Small' can be really tiny!

The idea is that the big one is the parental figure and stays with the child. Similarly the small one, representing the child, travels with the parent.

This kind of message helps children to know that they are not the only ones who are missing their mum or dad and it can be reassuring for a child to know that the parent feels apprehensive too. It is a similar concept to a teddy or security blanket given to a baby.

For younger children there is a book that can accompany this activity: *No Matter What* (see opposite and page 44) which talks about the characters 'Large' and 'Small'.

When I go to the Royal tomorrow I will take 'Small' with me. Every time I look at him I will think of you. I miss you when we're apart and 'Small' helps me to feel close to you. 'Big' can go to bed with you and when you look at him, you'll know I am thinking of you.

There are other ways to maintain connections when apart. For example, you could sew a kiss or other symbol discreetly inside a school jumper (for the child) and inside a pocket (for the parent) that can be pressed when a bit of comfort is required.

Or everyone in the family can have a special coin, token or key ring or mobile phone 'charm' that symbolises the links between parents and children even when apart.

The beautifully illustrated book *No Matter What* by Debi Gliori (1999) tells the story of 'Large' (a parental figure portrayed as an animal) and 'Small' the inquisitive offspring who is finding it hard to know just how grumpy he can be before 'Large' will stop loving him. The book takes the child on a gentle yet magical adventure of unconditional love. It culminates in allowing 'Small' to ask perhaps the biggest question of all.

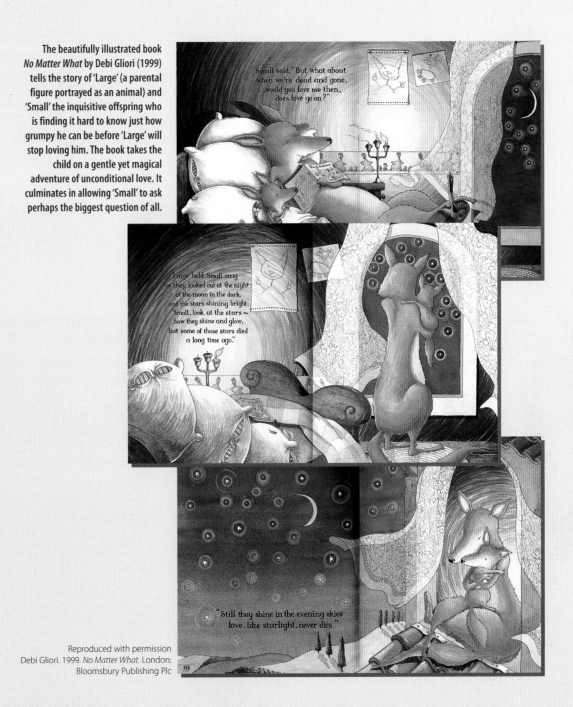

Night-time worries

Many children who feel burdened by the uncertainty that a serious illness can bring find it difficult to get to sleep; others find they are frequently woken by nightmares. Such disruption to sleep is particularly likely in a child who clams up by day and says they are OK, when in fact they may be holding on to a lot of concerns. A regular and secure bedtime routine will certainly help as well as some of the following ideas.

Snuggle blanket

Even a boisterous child can feel more secure swaddled in a cosy 'snuggle blanket'.

Accompanied by a regular bedtime story, the blanket becomes a subtle way to reinforce security and love. It even works well for older children who may choose to personalise the blanket their own way.

Worry dolls

Some children are helped by 'worry dolls' – a small bag of tiny people who carry a child's worries during the night to help the child sleep and feel less burdened by their worries. These can be found in some Oxfam or gift shops, bought online or you could make your own.

The child lays each worry doll on his or her pillow. They then pick them up, one at a time, and whisper a worry.

I am really worried that mum won't get better. Please look after that worry for me.

Then, one by one, they are placed back in the drawstring bag and placed under the pillow. The idea is that the worry dolls carry the child's worries through the night and work out ways for the child to feel stronger. Their use helps the child to put aside the concerns that prevent them from sleeping. Most importantly, it also helps adults to understand and talk about things that may be troubling a child.

Some children make worry fairies or superheroes using peg dolls.

I am really worried that dad may be too sick to go on holiday.

Dreamcatchers

The dreamcatcher is a Native American concept to protect the child while he or she sleeps. Folklore says that all the dreams and thoughts of the world flow over our head as we sleep. Bad dreams and thoughts are caught up in the web and only good dreams and thoughts filter down to the sleeping child through the feathers. Dreamcatchers can be bought online, in some gift shops, or you can make your own.

Hang the dreamcatcher above the child's bed and tell them the story, explaining how the web will capture the bad dreams. Help them believe that this may help with any nightmares or intrusive thoughts.

Beads woven into the web stand for 'heroes' or 'heroines' (real or imaginary) who can help keep the bad dreams away. Extra beads can be added for extra 'strength'. One child added beads representing Superman, Dr Who, David Beckham and his pet dog to his dreamcatcher as he felt he could trust these 'heroes' to overpower his feelings of helplessness and fear. Another child decided to put a sticker of his favourite team winning the FA Cup in the centre of the web.

Writing into the future

Writing down special memories and the thoughts you may have about the future can create a unique and special gift for your children. There are several ways to go about this. Initially it seems a daunting prospect, so don't feel you have to write everything at once. Some parents choose to write something every day; others write when they think of something they want to add.

Little box of big thoughts

The idea behind this activity is to write a series of cards to be kept together in a box. Post-it notes, postcards or small pieces of coloured paper can all be used and special sets of cards are available (see page 46).

On each card you write simple **thoughts**. Here are some starters:

I love you because …

I feel proud when you …

I hope that …

A favourite memory I have is …

You make me laugh when …

When we're not together, what I miss most about you is …

Remember when …

Thank you for …

The cards can be kept somewhere safe. You might want to keep them in a memory box.

The completed box is a unique and permanent reminder for your child that you and he/she share a secure and loving relationship – no matter what.

I wish box

This activity focuses on creating a set of **wishes** – made by a parent on behalf of their child. It is also another way of encouraging communication between a parent and child when someone is seriously ill.

You will need some small pieces of card and a box or bag to keep them in. Write a wish for your child on each piece of card. Here are examples of what other parents have written.

I wish ... that you will always remember just how much dad and I love you. Love mum x

I wish ... that you will learn to have great confidence in yourself. I have great confidence in you and always will. Love dad x

I wish ... that you will always feel OK about showing your feelings when you want to, with people you trust. Love mum x

I wish ... that you can grow up to be both strong and gentle, sensitive and tough, calm and emotional, serious and playful. Love dad x

I wish ... that you can forget the times we argued. I am so very proud of you and always will be. Love dad x

The wishes can then be rolled up and kept in a small 'wish box'. You may like to include a dandelion seed for each wish. You could then suggest to your children that they blow a dandelion clock sometimes to remember the wishes you have for them.

This is a lasting way to let a child know they are loved unconditionally and that a parent's love endures throughout serious illness.

"I'm not writing these wishes because I'm dying. I am alive and I want my kids to know I love them and don't want to leave them! It was hard at first as I didn't want to tempt fate, but now I feel relieved that they are there should the cancer come back." Diane

"I put it off for ages – partly because I thought I would soon get better and it wouldn't be necessary. As time wore on, I was getting worse and I decided to write some things down for Sam in a notebook. I really wanted him to know how proud I am of him and how much I hate being ill. When I got into it, I remembered all sorts of important and special times together. It was the hardest thing to write, thinking I might not be here to share this – some days I couldn't do it as it was just too upsetting. On other days it really perked me up. I try to think of Sam reading it when he is my age." Gita

Letters for the future

If your illness is progressing, it's very hard to accept that you may not live long enough to see your children growing up. But although you may not be there in person, you do have a chance to write letters remembering happy times you've spent together or looking ahead to their future lives.

Some parents are put off from doing this, because they think it will be too upsetting. Others worry that messages from the past could simply re-open old wounds and cause future pain for their children.

The reality is that parents generally do find it very difficult, but also very rewarding, to write such letters. As the quote on the left shows, remembering happy times and doing something positive for your children can lift your spirits and give you a sense of purpose. Although children may feel sad when they read such messages, they also say it makes them feel very loved that their parent could think ahead and do this for them.

The only real risk of letters like these is that children can feel they've been given a set of instructions which need to be followed out of respect for you. If you decide to write letters for their graduation, their marriage or the birth of their first child, it is important to emphasise that you are happy whatever path they have chosen so that they do not feel they've let you down if they don't go to university, choose not to marry or never have children.

This is the hardest letter you will ever need to write. Ideally, and if possible, personalise it to each child or write it jointly to all your children and make enough copies so they have one each.

Guidelines for writing the letter

- Tell them in a simple and straightforward way how you feel about them. Let them know that you love them and that you would do anything not to be in this position.
- Other things that you could include might be some reflections on your life growing up and some of your struggles and successes. Help them to understand the things that have helped you cope in life and to celebrate the things you value, such as hope, perseverance and courage.
- You may want to mention the memory box that you have been gathering together.
- Also mention people, or toys which can be relied on to provide comfort.
- If you are a mother who is ill, you may want to talk about their dad, and if you are a father who is ill, you may want to talk about their mum. You may also want to talk about other key people who will cherish your children on your behalf. You may even want to mention the future possibility that your partner may find a new partner.
- Encourage them to keep their dreams, treasure their memories and share their stories with people who can hear them.

It would be good to think that the children will never have to read your letter, but if they do, it will be a priceless treasure.

Dear Finn

This is the hardest letter I've ever written. There are so many things I want you to know — it's difficult to know where to start ...

I think the most important thing for you to always remember is that you have a dad who thinks you are THE VERY BEST! I have known you for 16 years and even though we don't always agree on everything (especially your taste in music!) I am so proud to have you as my son. Right now, things do not look great in terms of my health. The doctors feel that I am unlikely to get better, even with this strong chemo ... so my future is uncertain. I feel so very angry that I may not be here to share the rest of your growing up years. I have had a lot of time to think lately and I realise that life is for living so I hope we will make the most of our time together.

Know that somehow life goes on and we will remain close to each other - wherever we might be.

Son - I'll always love you, no matter what. Never forget that.

Dad x x

A father wrote this letter to his son as he started a tough treatment regime. He gave it to him with a memory box. It showed a photo of them together on the top and the box was filled with holiday photos, certificates of both of their sporting achievements and a bottle of his favourite aftershave. The letter said it all and enabled the father and son to feel closer than they had in a long time.

I think the most important thing for you to always remember is that you have a dad who thinks you are THE VERY BEST!

This letter is from a single mother writing to her eight-year-old daughter, Sarah. This letter had been written and filed away for 11 months. It was given to Sarah by her guardians, Susan and Dan, after her mother died and is now kept safely in her memory box.

Dear Sarah

I am so, so, so, so sorry that you are reading this letter - I hoped you would never have to. I wish with all my heart that I was still alive and still with you and we could go on with our lives together.

You have been the most wonderful, marvellous, amazing daughter!! I have loved every single moment of being your mother and feel immensely proud to have you as my daughter.

I know you will be feeling sad. Desperately sad. You've had too much death in your life - too much death of those you love - grandpa, Bramble, Shelly-Hamster and the other animals. It's not fair on you - but please know that it's not something you are causing, it's just terribly unfair.

Please don't be afraid to love people in the future. It's the best thing to do! I wish I could be there now to comfort you. Isn't it sad that the one person who might be able to make it better is the one person who's made it worse?

Cry all you can. Hug Big Ted and Liddly and sob. Hug humans too. Susan and Dan, and grandma are all good for hugs. And when the time comes to stop crying - and it will - please stop. Don't feel bad about stopping, it's the right thing after a while. Please don't be sad for a long time ... remember the happy times instead.

Remember all the good times. All the fun. All the love. We've had such good, good times, haven't we? Times at home with pets and toys and water fights and snuggles on the sofa. Times away on holiday. Times just travelling along in the car chatting.

Talk about me a lot! Not in a sad way but just keep remembering some funny and ordinary things - and then talk about them. I've written some memories down but I know you'll think of loads more.

Some days won't be as good as others. You might feel angry, lonely, afraid, confused. Talk to other people about how you feel. There are two things that worry me ... one is that you might feel uncomfortable about some of the times when we've argued. Sarah, listen to me ... forget this. It's not important. All that's important is how much we loved each other (and we really did) and all the goodness and joy we had between us.

The other thing that concerns me is your occasional lack of confidence and belief in yourself - like when you say you don't want to do something because you might fail. Please remember that you are a unique and amazing individual. And you are full of loving ways. I love your creativity and enthusiasm. For my sake, please remember that you are wonderful - all the best of things rolled up in one special daughter.

I hope the rest of your life is everything you want it to be. Tough stuff can and will happen and I know you will find ways to survive, be strong and learn. Susan and Dan will be great people to grow up with, lean on, rely on (and argue with sometimes!) I hope you will have a group of special friends to trust and eventually someone special to love. I hope you find work that satisfies and nourishes you. I hope your dreams come true - whatever they may be. And on the special days of your life, remember me and know that I am so proud of you and I am surrounding you with my love.

It has been wonderful to share these years with you. I'm so sorry I couldn't stay. I'd have done anything to be able to. My love for you is so strong - nothing can break it, certainly not something as insignificant as death. My love will surround you, protect you, nourish you and support you all the days of your life.

Remember me, love me, love others, love yourself - I love you forever.

Mum x x x x x x

Sources of information and support

Here are some sources of support – for parents and for children – which you may want to call on from time to time.

The contacts below concentrate on supporting a child when a parent has cancer. There are other organisations that can help when a parent is seriously ill with other conditions, for example MS, MND or AIDS.

Similarly, all children's hospices now offer services to the siblings of children in their care. They should be able to offer helpful resources – or contact the Association of Children's Hospices (www.childhospice.org.uk).

Helplines and e-mail support for parents

Winston's Wish

Support, guidance and information from experienced professionals for anyone (parents, family and professionals) who is concerned about a child facing the death of a family member or who has already been bereaved.
Helpline: 08452 03 04 05 – open Monday to Friday, 9am to 5pm
E-mail: info@winstonswish.org.uk
www.winstonswish.org.uk
www.winstonswish.org.uk/foryoungpeople – an interactive website for young people

Cancerbackup

Europe's leading cancer information charity, offering up-to-date cancer information, practical advice and support for cancer patients, their families and carers. Helpline support is offered in 13 languages.
Helpline: 0808 800 1234 – open Monday to Friday, 9am to 8pm
E-mail: info@cancerbackup.org
www.cancerbackup.org.uk

Macmillan Cancer Support

Macmillan provides practical, medical, emotional and financial support and campaigns for better cancer care.
Helpline: 0808 808 2020 – open Monday to Friday, 9am to 10pm
E-mail: cancerline@macmillan.org.uk
www.macmillan.org.uk

Cancer Counselling Trust

The Cancer Counselling Trust is unique in providing free, specialist counselling for anyone affected by cancer, across the UK.
Helpline: 020 7704 1137 – there is an answering machine when the office is closed
E-mail: support@cctrust.org.uk
www.cctrust.org.uk

Parentline Plus

Parentline Plus provides support over the phone and useful resources on all issues concerned with parenting.
Helpline: 0808 800 2222 – open 24 hours a day, 7 days a week
www.parentlineplus.org.uk

Samaritans

Provides confidential non-judgemental support, 24 hours a day for people experiencing feelings of distress or despair, including those which could lead to suicide.
Helpline: 08457 90 90 90 – open 24 hours a day, 7 days a week
E-mail: jo@samaritans.org
www.samaritans.org.uk

Tak Tent Cancer Support – Scotland

Promotes care for people on the cancer journey, and their families and friends, by providing emotional support to all.
Helpline: 0141 211 0122 – open Monday to Friday, 10am to 3pm
E-mail: tak.tent@care4free.net
www.taktent.org

Tenovus Cancer Information Centre – Wales

A charitable organisation committed to the control of cancer through quality research, prevention education, counselling and patient care.
Helpline: 0808 808 1010 – open Monday to Friday, 9am to 5pm
www.tenovus.com

Ulster Cancer Foundation – Northern Ireland

Northern Ireland's leading local cancer charity, dedicated to helping save lives and enhancing the quality of life of everyone affected by cancer. The UCF has staff able to train others in a pioneering support programme for children whose parents or siblings have cancer 'CLIMB' (Children's Lives Involve Moments of Bravery). For further information on CLIMB see www.childrenstreehousefdn.org

Helpline: 0800 783 3339 – open Monday to Friday, 9am to 5pm
E-mail: infocis@ulstercancer.org
www.ulstercancer.org

Helplines for children and young people

ChildLine

ChildLine is the free helpline for children and young people in the UK. Children and young people can talk to counsellors about any problem.

Helpline: 0800 1111 – open 24 hours a day, 7 days a week
www.childline.org.uk

Cruse

Support for young people after someone has died.

Young Persons Freephone Helpline: 0808 808 1677 – open Monday to Friday, 9.30am to 5pm
E-mail: info@rd4u.org.uk
www.rd4u.org.uk

Get Connected

Provides a free, confidential helpline that gives young people in difficult situations the support and information they need to decide what they want to happen next. It could be anything from a listening ear to somewhere safe to stay for the night.

Helpline: 0808 808 4994 – open 7 days a week, 1pm to 11pm
E-mail: help@getconnected.org.uk
www.getconnected.org.uk

Macmillan Youth Line

Macmillan supports young people (aged 12 to 21) who are affected by cancer – either that of a family member or if they are ill themselves.

Helpline: 0808 808 0800 – open Monday to Friday, 9am to 10pm
E-mail: youthline@macmillan.org.uk
www.macmillan.org.uk

Useful websites

As well as the organisations listed above, here are some other websites which you might find useful.

www.macmillan.org.uk/whybother/index.html

Why bother finding out more about cancer? Because over one million people in the UK have been diagnosed with cancer, so a lot of children and young people will know someone affected by it.

www.riprap.org.uk

This website can help children and young people cope when a parent has cancer. There are stories from other young people going through the same situations. The website has information and tips to help children understand and deal with what is going on in their family.

www.siblinks.org

The aim is to provide a network for young people (aged 13 to 25) who have or have had a family member affected by cancer to gain support through social, practical and emotional activities and provide information to raise awareness.

www.winstonswish.org.uk

Winston's Wish offers practical support and guidance to families, professionals and anyone concerned about a child when someone is seriously ill or when someone important has died.

Helpful books for children

There are many excellent books for children. Here are a few of our favourites.

Ask Me
Antje Damm
Frances Lincoln Children's Books, 2005
ISBN 978-1-84507-386-2

This book offers an engaging way for primary school aged children to generate those really special conversations that happen when the defences are down and a child feels more able to open up. When you ask a child "What did you do at school today?" the answer is often "Not much". However, if you say "What questions did you ask, or want to ask today?", it takes the child's mind to a different, more interesting, thoughtful and curious place.

Flamingo Dream
Donna Jo Napoli
Illustrated by Cathie Felstead
Greenwillow Books, 2002
ISBN 0-688-17863-4

This bright and colourful book is narrated by a young boy whose dad is seriously ill and dies soon after a trip to Florida to see the place where he grew up. The collage style illustrations capture the things the boy collects to remind him of his dad. This is a sensitive but honest book, which emphasises the importance of memories.

The Huge Bag of Worries
Virginia Ironside
Hodder Wayland, 1998
ISBN 0-750026391

This book relates the simple story of a girl who finds she is carrying an ever growing 'bag of worries'. Eventually she receives help to share the worries with others. This book is a very useful starter to conversations with children under 11 about anxieties and concerns.

My Mommy Has Cancer
Carolyn Stearns-Parkinson
Park Press, 1991
ISBN 0963028707

This is an American story book about a child whose mother is in hospital for treatment for cancer. Suitable for use with children aged from three to six.

No Matter What
Debi Gliori
Bloomsbury Publishing, 1999
ISBN 0-747581347

This book gently and powerfully conveys the idea of unconditional parental love through the characters of Large and Small. It supports the concept of 'Big' and 'Small' described on page 32 and is suitable for children aged from three to eight.

On Eagles' Wings
Sue Mayfield
Lion Hudson, 2004
ISBN 0-745948901

Tony's mother is dying. There's nothing he can do about it and he can't always put a brave face on things. Often he wishes he could just fly away from everything, like an eagle, powerful and free. Gradually, through his experiences, Tony begins to understand that death can sometimes bring freedom. A very readable and sensitive story about growing up, family relationships and facing bereavement.

There's NO Such Thing as a Dragon

Jack Kent

Golden Books, 1975

ISBN 0-375832084

This is another really helpful story for children aged from four to eight. It is a funny, quirky story about a little dragon that gets bigger – eventually becoming an overwhelming size because no-one is noticing him. It subtly conveys to a child that even tough stuff can and needs to be talked about to make it more manageable.

The Secret C: Straight Talking About Cancer

Julie Stokes OBE

Winston's Wish/Macmillan Cancer Relief, 2000

Second Edition 2009

ISBN 978-0-9559539-2-7

Available from Winston's Wish on 01242 515157 or www.winstonswish.org.uk/shop

This book aims to help children ask questions about cancer and answers some common questions. It has a simple description of what cancer is and the treatments. The book discusses side-effects in easy to understand language as well as the emotions that a child may have when a family member has cancer. Suitable for use with children aged from four to 11.

When Someone Has a Very Serious Illness

Marge Heegaard

Fairview Press, 1993

ISBN 0 96205 024 5

This workbook aims to help children understand their feelings when someone in their family is seriously ill.

When Your Mum or Dad Has Cancer

Ann Couldrick

Sobell Publications, 1991

ISBN 978-0951753736

Single copies available from Cancerbackup on 0808 800 1234.

This booklet for children uses simple cartoons to explain cancer, treatment and common feelings children may have. Suitable for use with children aged from three to eight.

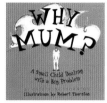

Why Mum?

Catherine Thornton

Veritas Publications 2005

ISBN: 1 85390 891 6

A book which is useful for a child aged 8 to 13 to talk about the impact of cancer treatment on family life. Sometimes Mum or Dad can become ill and this can be a difficult time for the whole family; Matthew was seven when his mum discovered she had a disease called cancer. She had to go into hospital and Matthew was very worried about her. It was a difficult year for everybody, but after receiving special treatment from doctors and nurses she got better and could play with Matthew again.

Useful resources

Resources available from Winston's Wish

Many of the items referred to in this booklet can be purchased through the Winston's Wish website – www.winstonswish.org.uk/shop – or from our resources catalogue (call 01242 515157 for a copy).

Memory boxes
We have developed three unique designs which will appeal to different children.

Little Box of Big Thoughts
A box with a variety of cards; some are simply blank, others have helpful prompts like "I love you because ..." This is a simple way to create meaningful memories of important relationships.

Other resources

Memory book template
A memory book template which can be completed and placed in a child's memory book can be downloaded from the Remember Me When I'm Gone website (www.remembermewhenimgone.org).

Memory books
Priceless Treasures (www.pricelesstreasuresonline.com) produces a range of memory books for parents and grandparents to complete as a record of things and people who give meaning to their life.

Winston's Wish

Winston's Wish began in 1992 out of concern to provide continuing support for children whose parents were referred to palliative care and oncology teams.

Seventeen years on, we are the leading childhood bereavement charity and the largest provider of services to bereaved families in the UK. We operate the national helpline (08452 03 04 05) for anyone concerned about a child who has been bereaved or who is facing the possible death of a family member. We have a comprehensive and interactive website which includes activities for children, produce award-winning publications, and conduct training and consultancy for professionals.

These activities are informed by our direct experience of supporting children and families individually and in residential groups. We offer specialist groups for those bereaved through suicide, and for those bereaved through murder.

Our work also brings us into contact with children and adults who are facing the serious illness of a family member.

A big thank you

We would like to say a heartfelt thank you to all the families from whom we learn something new every day. We regularly hear from adults who, as children, felt excluded from their parent's illness. We now have an opportunity to do things differently – giving parents an emotional 'first aid kit' to use with the people they love most – their children. We believe that what happens before the death of a parent can have a profound and positive effect on the child's resilience afterwards.

In 2007, we contributed to a groundbreaking Channel 4 television series called 'The Mummy Diaries'. Our thanks to Sue Murphy, Commissioning Editor Channel 4 Television; Emma Westcott, Executive Producer; Amanda Blue, Series Producer/Director; and Hannah Runham, Assistant Producer.

The films aimed to help people understand how ordinary families can cope with the extraordinary situations that arise when the mother has advanced cancer. These families' experiences have informed much of the content of this booklet – they are the experts who intuitively knew what was right for their children and we thank them for their insights. Together they demonstrate that there really is no right or wrong way to do it – just an openness to allow children to be part of the way forward.